Overcoming Deptostrofy

A Complete Guide to Debt and Loans Management for Free Life Forever and Ever

Table of Contents

Introduction **8**

Part 1: How Do People Get Into Debt? **9**

  Chapter 1: Causes of Debt 9

    Types of Debt 10

    How To Know You're In Debt.. 11

    Good vs. Bad Debts 13

    Good Debt 13

    Risks of Good Debts.. 14

    Bad Debts 15

    Are These Good or Bad? 16

    Money and Marriage... 17

  Chapter 2: Stop Accumulating Debt and Loans Starting NOW! **21**

    Get Educated on Debt 21

    Health... 23

Part 2: Organize Your Debt **25**

  Chapter 3: Assess Your Situation......................... **25**

    Making Sure You Are Honest 25

    The Mental Pain of Analyzing Your Financial Situation... 25

    Assessing How Much Debt You Owe........................... 26

    Assessing Your Credit Card Debt 26

Assessing Living Situation Debt 26

Student Loan Debt 27

Government Debt 27

Putting It All Together 27

Escaping Credit Card Disaster 28

Charge Cards 28

Chapter 4: The Benefits of Money Management– Stopping the Madness 30

Conscious Thought vs. Reactive Spending 30

Budgets: An Introduction 30

Basic Benefits of Budgeting 31

Regaining Control 31

Strategically Coping With Deptostrofy 32

A Savings Plan 32

Capping Impulse Spending 33

Goal Achievement 34

Ultimate Benefit: MORE Money 34

Chapter 5: How to Recognize Bad Advice 35

It's Your Last Great Tax Write-Off 35

Interest Deduction 36

Conflicts Of Interest 40

Chapter 6: New Perspectives on Debt and Housing 44

Owning Too Much House Can Cripple Your Finances .. 44

A Few House-Buying Tips 45

Debt is Often an Unnecessary Risk 46

What If you're Drowning in Debt? 51

Part 3: Setting Financial Goals 53

Chapter 7: Make Your Plan 53

Make Sure You Have Explored All Your Options........... 53

Analyzing Your Income 53

Analyzing Your Expenses 54

Add in the Debt 54

Setting Aside a Fixed Number to Allocate to
Your Debt 55

Deciding Which Debt to Pay Off First 55

Setting A Time Frame 56

What If I Don't Have Extra Cash To Allocate To Debt? . 56

Create A New Financial System 57

Create A Budget 57

Emergency Fund 58

Monthly Financial System 58

Part 4: Taking Action 62

Chapter 8: Investing: The Secret to Financial Freedom... 62

Types of Investments 62

What is an Ownership Investment? 62

What is Lending Investment? 64

Chapter 9: Start Building Your Credit.................. 65

What Determines Your Credit Card Limit? 65

No-Limit Cards Are False 66

What You Can Do to Improve Your Credit Limit 67
Ask For an Increase on Your Credit Limit 68
What to Consider Before Asking 68
The Process of Asking 68

Conclusion 71

Text Copyright © David Stokes

All rights reserved. No part of this guide may be reproduced in any form without permission in writing from the publisher except in the case of brief quotations embodied in critical articles or reviews.

Legal & Disclaimer

The information contained in this book and its contents is not designed to replace or take the place of any form of medical or professional advice; and is not meant to replace the need for independent medical, financial, legal or other professional advice or services, as may be required. The content and information in this book have been provided for educational and entertainment purposes only.

The content and information contained in this book have been compiled from sources deemed reliable, and it is accurate to the best of the Author's knowledge, information, and belief. However, the Author cannot guarantee its accuracy and validity and cannot be held liable for any errors and/or omissions. Further, changes are periodically made to this book as and when needed. Where appropriate and/or necessary, you must consult a professional (including but not limited to your doctor, attorney, financial advisor or such other professional advisor) before using any of the suggested remedies, techniques, or information in this book.

Upon using the contents and information contained in this book, you agree to hold harmless the Author from and against any damages, costs, and expenses, including any legal fees potentially resulting from the application of any of the information provided by this book. This disclaimer applies to any loss, damages or injury caused by the use and application, whether directly or indirectly, of any advice or information presented, whether for breach of contract, tort, negligence, personal injury, criminal intent, or under any other cause of action. You agree to accept all risks of using the information presented in this book.

You agree that by continuing to read this book, where appropriate and/or necessary, you shall consult a professional (including but not limited to your doctor, attorney, or financial advisor or such other advisor as needed) before using any of the suggested remedies, techniques, or information in this book.

Introduction

Debt and loans remain an issue that plagues the people of several of the world's developed nations as people believe it is now harder and harder to make payments plus interest on income they borrowed. Traditional financial planners, conventional wisdom, the media, and frequently our families, inform us that it will take determination, superior file- self-discipline and maintaining to overcoming Deptostrofy. Surely to become debt-free initially, maybe these characteristics alone could make a difference. However, they fail for anyone attempting to stay debt-free long term. That is another story altogether.

The secret ingredient? Knowledge. Knowledge is power. A thinking process makes all the difference in money and income. It fuels the continued inspiration we all need to do whatever it takes to remain debt-free. Such knowledge exists today in easy-to-comprehend language for anyone who seeks it.

Part 1: How Do People Get Into Debt?

Chapter 1: Causes of Debt

Debt is often defined as the amount owed by a person to a lender or creditor. Millions of people are struggling daily to avoid and overcome deptostrofy, but millions of people are at the same time succumbing in indebtedness. We are always longing for the day that we can become free from debt in our lives and enjoy the benefits of financial freedom.

However, before we start learning the solution, we must first know what the problem is and what its causes are. We will start our journey to financial freedom by understanding why people have debts and how these arise.

"The first reason why you have debt is because of... Money"

1. Spending More Than You Earn

For most people, the main reason why they are in debt is because of money, more specifically, spending more money than they are earning. Overspending is one of the main reasons why people go into debt. In the United States, more than 40% of Americans have outstanding debts due to living beyond their means.

This is aggravated more due to the credit system, which has enticed millions of people to use credit cards instead of cash to pay for their purchases. Credit cards and loan offers such as payday loans and the like, give people the chance to "buy now and pay later" which is the main ingredient for debt. This overspending habit will lead to the next reason why people have debts.

2. Misuse of Credit and Loan Systems

Most developed countries have a stable credit system. Though the developed credit system can benefit people in many ways, it is also a double-edged sword, which can easily cast anyone into the abyss of debt.

The idea of "paying later" gives people the courage to spend without thinking about any unforeseen events that may happen in the future that may cause their finances to break down and lead them crashing into bankruptcy. Though the system of credit and loan systems have benefits, their misuse can create a whole load of trouble.

3. Improper Lifestyle

Bad money management is the next thing that causes people to get in and stay in debt. Bad lifestyle choices and poor money handling will undoubtedly make people wallow in debt.

Gambling, a luxurious lifestyle and indulging in excesses will surely drain a person's economic potential and thus force them to get loans or use credit. A lot of people get plunged into deptostrofy, which could have been avoided if only their money and resources were used properly.

Another thing that makes people become overshadowed by debt is they are too lazy to work in the first place. It is important to know that working and not becoming lazy is an integral part of our ideas concerning the reasons why people have debts.

4. Sudden Emergencies

The last thing that plunges people into debt is sudden emergencies. Accidents, loss of jobs, calamities, disabilities and such are all factors that can create insurmountable debts. These are the four main reasons why people are plunged into debt and suffer every single problem that goes with it.

Types of Debt

As much as all debts are about borrowing money from a different source, there are good debts and bad debts. Good debts are debts that are taken to help you manage your finances considerably.

Examples of good debts are:

- Taking a mortgage loan- The beauty of having a mortgage loan is that the value appreciates and you may make money in the long run. The other benefit is that in the case of taking a commercial premise, you will have rent paid to you as you continue servicing your loan.
- An education loan.
- A business loan –taking a loan to build wealth helps in increasing your stream of income.
- A loan for a rainy day.

While the above kinds of debts can be good because of the intentions and the bigger picture, interest rates and late payment habits can make them bad debts. One should always check the amount of debt they have before piling on debt after debt.

Bad debts, on the other hand, are pretty much the opposite of good debts. When good debts are secured with a very long repayment period these should be considered a bad debt. This is because you will end up paying higher interest rates. It is also wise to consider the percentage of debt versus your income. This will tell you whether your debt is good or bad. Any debt that does not help you grow your wealth is a bad debt. Credit cards are a good example of bad debts.

How To Know You're In Debt

Not beating the deadline to meeting your bills.

It is that day of the month when you should be meeting your bills like your mortgage, water bill, power bill, labor and all other sorts of recurring monthly bills. Then you realize that not only are you struggling to pay, but you're a month or two behind on payment. When lucky and not behind, you still make the payment late. You're in deep my friend!

Don't pick up calls.

Are there times that your phone will ring endlessly without you getting it? Or you see the caller ID and decide not to pick because you know you owe the caller money? Say no more.

Cannot access funds from financial institutions.

You're denied a top-up to a loan you have with a financial institution, and, all you get after an application for more credit is rejection letters. This means that your credit score is leaving you with no access to more funds.

Your debts have debts.

This has got to be the worst kind of debt. Where you get money from source A to settle a debt with source B. It even gets worse if these debts have interest attached to them. If you're doing that right now it's time to have a sit down with yourself and critically think about a way out of this. Luckily for you, being on here is one step closer to getting out.

You want to go crazy at the mention/sight of money.

Ever been so hungry that you salivated at the thought of food. Even the food that you ordinarily wouldn't eat much? Like a platter of greasy fries with leftover salsa salad? Well, you can relate. This is how it feels when you are knee deep in debt and you see someone spending money. Everyone's spending at such a time seems irrelevant.

Being in denial and secretive when money is discussed.

Sometimes a spouse may borrow money with the partner being in the dark. This spouse will do whatever it takes to keep it a secret. Answering calls outside the room and hiding their pay slip/financial statements are some of the things one will do to keep it under wraps. This is so tasking!!!!

Most (if not all) of your income goes to paying debts.

Payday is finally here and you sit down to plan. Obviously, being the good planner you are, you prioritize the settling of debts. Then you get to the bottom-line. There is very little to nothing left after this.

Good vs. Bad Debts

You have to look at the types of debts you have and what needs to be covered first. Part of this includes looking at the good debts that you have. Owing good debts will not be as harmful to your credit report as the bad debts. You still have to pay them off just like you do with every other debt. However, those good debts are not ones that you have to pay off right away.

You must resolve the bad debts including the unsecured debts before you consider paying off the good debts if possible. Having a credit report that includes more good debts than bad debts is always good.

Good Debt

A good debt is one that helps you build the assets you have. With good debt, you are producing income while also expanding your net worth.

There are many types of good debts:

1. Real Estate Investments

Real estate investments include not only any properties you live in but also your business properties or any properties around the world that you have a stake in. People often use these real estate properties for years before they sell them, possibly at a profit.

Of course, many people may rent out those properties as a means of making an income, especially since the home rental and vacation rental industry has been blossoming. The expenses associated with these real estate investments often include mortgage payments, homeowners' insurance costs, and maintenance charges.

2. Investments

Investments include many debts relating to stocks, commodities, currencies, bonds, precious metals, futures, and many other things you might be interested in. These investments can produce great profits over time, but they may also be risky. Some investments may be even riskier than others, particularly alternative investments that are not as widely followed as other options.

You might contribute a certain amount of money to an IRA every year. The thousands of dollars you spend on this investment is a good debt because you are working to get your IRA to grow in value over time.

3. Small Business Functions

The expenses associated with owning and operating a business can be high and may include charges relating to renting a property, maintaining an inventory, marketing, managing employees, and so forth. The charges associated with running a small business are interpreted as good debts.

4. Educational Expenses

Educational expenses involved with attending college or receiving training to earn a degree, certification are considered good debts because they will help you to potentially earn even more money through the newfound credentials or experience.

These good debts still need to be paid off like with any other debt, but not as quickly as bad debts.

Risks of Good Debts

Although the good debts that you come across are beneficial, there are plenty of concerns that should be considered.

- The high cost of a real estate investment could be too high when the expenses associated with running it are considered. The fact that these will continue throughout the life of your investment might prove to be a challenge to manage.

- There is a chance that your stock investments or real estate investments might lose value. The markets for all of these are unpredictable and challenging.
- Every small business runs the same risk of failure as a large business.
- Increasing your education might not work as well as you might wish due to a difficult job market, changes in trends, difficulties with relocating, and so forth.

You have to look at what you're going to get out of any good debt to know if and how it will be a financial benefit to you.

Bad Debts

Bad debts are the debts that need to be paid off first. You must make sure they are resolved first as they will do more to hurt your credit rating. The following are examples of bad debts:

1. Consumable Goods

These are best described as the debts incurred on your credit and charge cards. The biggest problem with the debts that involve consumable goods is that they are not going to last forever, hence the name.

It should also be noted that the value of consumable goods is often considered to be about half of what was paid for them. Clothes wear out and food gets eaten, for instance.

2. Credit Card Debts

Consumable goods can make up a sizable portion of your credit card debts. Anything that you put on your credit cards can be bad debts. This is due to how credit card debts are typically unsecured. The interest rates on credit cards are often much higher than other loans.

3. Cars

Most people need a car to get around, especially if you have a job that requires you to travel. The problem is that a car can be seen as a bad debt for the following reasons:

- The interest charges on a car loan can be high. This is assuming you have a car loan.
- Insurance costs can be rather high. You cannot go without car insurance as it is required by law. If you get into an accident or you encounter some trouble like a traffic violation while on the road, your insurance premiums can be affected.
- Oil, gas, tires, and general maintenance can be a burden.
- Your car's value will always depreciate. Depreciation begins immediately after you buy the car.

Paying off the entire car loan is clearly the best idea to avoid interest charges. You could always consider a less costly used vehicle as the depreciation will be significantly lower.

Are These Good or Bad?

This next section is devoted to certain debts that might be either good or bad. You might find that they are useful for many things in your life, but that does not mean each of them is a necessity.

1. Investment Borrowing

You might need to borrow some money to purchase an investment. The borrowing process requires leverage. This occurs when you are borrowing money with the intention of investing that money. The leveraged money will be borrowed with a low rate of interest. Meanwhile, the money will be invested in something with the potential of it having a higher rate of return.

This could be interesting for your investments, but there is the chance that your investment will drop in value, although that can be said for just about anything you might invest in.

2. Consolidation Loans

A consolidation loan takes many debts you have and combines them into one loan. This may include a lower interest rate. Consolidation will be discussed later in this guide.

3. Credit Card Rewards

One of the top reasons why so many people open credit card accounts is because of the rewards. From frequent flyer miles to cash back offers, there are many things that you might come across when getting a credit card to work for you.

That does not mean every credit card is going to be worthwhile. You should consider the risks associated with the credit card you are going to use. More importantly, you have to consider how often you plan to use the card.

The main goal for your debts is to make sure the bad ones are paid off first.

Money and Marriage

Today, many tell us money is the number one problem causing divorce. We know the Bible speaks more about money, possessions, materialism and the proper use or improper use of money than almost any other subject.

A simple review of a Bible Concordance on these issues will prove my point: The average married couple in the year 2017 owed more than $15,000 in credit card debt. With the good economy that year, it is a contradiction to see bankruptcies were nearly 800,000. There were more than 1,000,000 bankruptcies granted in the year 2014.

We need to ask ourselves: What is the cause of all these financial problems? Why do couples struggle with finances? Why are our couples getting deeper in debt with no plan to change? Let's work on the problem of debt. Ironically, the solution is found in my acronym: D.E.B.T.

- Discipline
- Energy
- Budget
- Trust

DISCIPLINE in a couple's finances is the basis for healthy finances. This applies to anyone. Proverbs 12:1 (NIV) reads: Whoever loves discipline loves knowledge, but he who hates correction is stupid.

Some Bible translations are direct, and this is one of them. A marriage without financial discipline is a marriage facing possible severe difficulty. As this translation points out, it's stupid to avoid correction, instruction, and discipline. Money in a marriage without discipline is a recipe for a financial tsunami.

Sooner or later financial woes will flood into our marriage and when it does, the marriage may be destroyed. Our financial failure impacts our children, friends, and family. The word discipline is so important, I have dedicated the last chapter in this book to the benefits of discipline. To become debt free will require discipline.

ENERGY exists in all marriages. The problem is, the energy may be spent in the wrong direction. Couples have energy to work, to have fun, go on vacations, bear children, and enjoy the physical rewards of marriage. The energy we use to shop for things like work, cars, furniture, homes, clothes, and material possessions is usually our biggest use of energy.

If we could direct, guide, or monitor some of our energy toward making sound financial decisions, we would surely see greater financial success. As couples, we should place our energy in praying together about our spending, in reading the Word of God and in seeking His help in financial decisions.

The energy we have to make money comes from the Lord. Deuteronomy 8:18 (NIV) reads: But remember the Lord your God for it is He who gives you the ability to produce wealth.

Energy is wonderful, yet it needs to be directed and brought under control. Couples should ask the Lord to direct them and agree together to focus some of their energy to become debt-free.

BUDGET. Everyone knows a budget is critical in marriage. Proverbs 16 –9 (NKJV) reads: A man's heart plans his way. But the Lord directs his steps.

This shows the importance of making an effort to plan our finances through the tool of a budget. The budget is the place where a husband and wife come together to plan how they will use the income God provides. Doing a budget may be the only time a couple will sit down and plan the use of money.

My experience shows only five percent of the couples I've interviewed have had such a meeting. A well-planned budget requires input by both the husband and wife. Both must openly discuss their wants, needs, and desires. Both must listen and put others' needs above their own personal wants, needs, and desires.

When it comes to spending, wives are often confronted by their husband for buying lots of little things for the home or for the children and when these purchases are not planned, they put pressure on the budget. On the other hand, traditionally, men are usually the ones who make the big spending decisions. A husband may argue with his wife over the $20 and $30 purchases she makes on the family or the house. Yet, the same men go out and buy a $55,000 recreation vehicle and put a $700 car payment on a budget that is struggling. I am not making that up. Obviously it does not happen in all marriages.

In marriage we come together as one. We are decisions together, pray together, have fun together, laugh together, and cry together. Let's work toward preparing a budget and living within it. There is little hope for couples to live debt-free without a plan of monitored spending. AKA, a budget.

TRUST. My favorite scripture about trust is found in Proverbs 3:5 (NKJV) reads: Trust in the Lord with all your heart and lean not on your own understanding.

I realize I quote this quite often. But it is a scripture that must be part of our daily life.

Once, I interviewed a couple who were planning to get married. They wanted to know how to set up their finances for the change from being single to being married. The first thing I suggested was to set up a joint checking account. When the guy heard my advice, he said, "How do I know I can trust her?" He wanted to marry her and yet it scared him to death to put his paycheck in the same account where she could write checks. How do you think that made her feel? It's obvious they had never discussed this issue.

We all know trust is vital in a marriage, both husband and wife must earn each other's trust. By the way, that couple decided to delay their wedding until they could work out the problem. About six months later they were married in our church. I thank the Lord they settled this issue before the wedding.

A marriage without trust is a marriage headed for failure. I've said this before but it is worth saying over and over again. We all trust the Lord, or at least we all say we trust Him. The bigger question is: does God trust us in our finances?

The acronym D.E.B.T. can be an important tool in dealing with financial decisions in marriage. Without Discipline, Energy, a Budget and Trust we will all end up with DEBT. However, when couples receive the discipline of the Lord, focus their energy, prepare a budget, trust the Lord, debt-free living will be their reward.

My prayer for all married couples is: "Heavenly Father, you ordained marriage. Your word tells us when we are married we become one flesh. We must come together in our thinking and decision making. Lord, help all married couples to become united in their desire to seek your help in every area of life. We believe you want us to be free from debt. May married couples join together in their desire to be debt-free. In Jesus' name we pay. Amen."

Chapter 2: Stop Accumulating Debt and Loans Starting NOW!

I'm sure you're very excited to get stuck into this book and learn how you can apply this system to get out of debt in one of the quickest ways possible, however, to achieve this goal effectively there are certain things you must do first!

This book is about ending bad financial habits and replacing them with good financial habits.

You've been digging a fatal hole of debt for yourself for however long those credit cards (or whatever it is) have been abused and it's now time to stop. For this system to work, no more debt can be accumulated!

If this means you have to cut your credit cards, then cut them!

If this means you have to freeze your credit cards, then freeze them!

Do whatever it takes so that you stop getting into more debt from this point forward.

From now on, whenever you are making purchases or paying bills, you do it with cash or a debit card (for those that don't know, a debit card is a card that lets you access money directly from your bank account and many banks work with the major card providers, Visa and MasterCard – therefore, a debit card can give you identical accessibility as a credit card, without the surcharges).

Get Educated on Debt

Since the majority of this book is about educating you with a system that you can apply to deal with and eliminate Deptostrofy, I can only provide basic education on debt here.

I definitely recommend reading some further articles on debt to enhance your knowledge; however, the basics that you should know are below.

Debt relies strongly on the fact that we live busy lives and can get easily distracted. When we're distracted, debt can go undetected and we never really realize the situation we're actually in until it becomes a bit too late.

It's a way for us to make a problem go away from the present moment, thinking that we can worry about it later.

But the truth is that it will never go away; debt just becomes a bigger and bigger worry the longer it stays in our lives.

The thing is that it's so common today that most people don't even realize it's a problem in the first place, so when they are struggling with payments later in their lives it can scare them!

We don't really learn much about money, specifically about debt, interest rates, bank accounts, financial instruments, saving for retirement, etc.

These are things that affect everyone at some point in their lives. Even if you have never had a credit card in your life and never get a home loan to buy a house, you still need some basic financial education because you have to put your money somewhere, and you also have to invest for your retirement.

Anyway, the point here is that debt relies on all of this and unfortunately it can really hurt us financially – which has the potential to lead into further problems like losing your house, your relationships, your job, and possibly leaving us with no other option except for bankruptcy. Something this powerful, I believe, should be taught to us at school!

Nevertheless, I congratulate you for reading this book now because I'm about to educate you like you've never been educated before. You're going to learn things you can apply to your life immediately. And best of all, you're going to start saying goodbye to debt forever!

Health

In this fast-paced society of ours, the convenience of take-out food is on the rise. Some people don't even know how to cook. If you eat out every day for breakfast, lunch, and dinner, you are spending your hard-earned dollars where instead you can be saving your wallet, saving your waistline, and saving your health.

Example.

Yes, eating that steak dinner at that fancy restaurant is delicious, and saves time on the food preparation and clean up. But that dinner cost at least $20 before taxes and tips. If you buy your own steak from the supermarket and prepare it yourself, you save a lot of money.

The added benefit of cooking your own food is you can control the amount of sugar, salt, MSG, oil, and other chemical substances entering your body, which can save your waistline and make you physically better looking. Your health improves too once you start preparing your own food.

Example.

When I started my job I decided to ask different colleagues out to lunch every day instead of bringing my own lunch. I believe it's important to get to know my colleagues so we can work better together.

After going a few weeks eating out every day, and I saw my credit card bill in the hundreds of dollars, I knew if I kept this up for months it would easily become very expensive. I won't be able to save money if I kept spending this way. Eating out once in a while is fine, but every day is too much.

TAKE ACTION!

For one month, try to cook all of your meals. There may be the occasional special occasion where you have to dine out, and that's okay. What you want to do is to form a habit. It takes a minimum of about 21 days, or 3 weeks to form a new habit.

When you cook your own food, you can have a more balanced meal. When you are eating food that has the right balance of carbohydrates, protein, fat, and the vitamins and minerals that your body needs, you'll actually feel better about herself and have higher self-esteem.

When you have higher self-esteem, you will be more confident in what you are able to do. You will have better energy levels, he will be sick less often, and you also experience less pain. Cooking your own food can also be fun.

Most important of all, you will be able to save on the money that you spent eating out. You won't have to pay to tips as if you were eating out. Basic groceries are also often exempt from taxes.

I also find that by learning to cook my own food, my knowledge of food increases, which is often a very good source of conversation topic. There is one common topic that almost every single person can talk about, and that is food.

You will also know more about health and nutrition; this will be able to help you have a healthier body. Also, by cooking your own food, you can tailor the food to your own tastes. You can also control the amount of food you eat. At a restaurant, you cannot control your food portions.

If you have food allergies, cooking your own food is the best way to control what goes into your diet. Things like nuts, Gluten which is a protein found in wheat, rye or barley can have serious implications on a person's immune system when they are absorbed by accident.

Part 2: Organize Your Debt

Chapter 3: Assess Your Situation

Before we can start hatching out a plan to get you out of deptostrofy, we first need to assess your current situation. You need to make sure that you are as detailed as possible when you are going over your current financial situation, and you need to make sure you have everything recorded. Nothing is worse than creating a plan to get out of debt, only to discover you have more debt then you planned for. This is a tough mental blow to handle. It's better to make sure you are extremely detailed in your assessment, no matter how bad it currently is. It's better to start from the bottom and claw your way up, rather than discover your situation is worse than you originally thought.

Making Sure You Are Honest

We mentioned above the importance of being honest with yourself when assessing your finances. This is key and you need to be able to be as specific and detailed as possible during this chapter. This will allow you to step back and really analyze and create a plan for your finances. You can create a plan to get out of any situation, so it's better to be honest even if you are in a lot of trouble. You are only hurting yourself if you hiding the facts about your true financial position.

The Mental Pain of Analyzing Your Financial Situation

Analyzing your financial situation and getting all your finances in order may cause you mental pain and anxiety. This is the number one reason why most people fail to create a plan. They would rather avoid this pain and hide their finances. If you are going to become debt free, you need to tackle this pain head on. No matter how painful your financial situation or how much anxiety you feel, you need to assess your situation if you are ever going to be debt free.

We recommend you choose a day and set aside a few hours to devote to assessing your finances. You can gather all your bills and financial statements and stick them in a folder until this time comes. When your day comes, remember to face the pain head on and remember the benefits of being debt free. This will allow you to stay focused and complete the first step to becoming debt free.

Assessing How Much Debt You Owe

One problem that people who have debt face is they don't know how much debt they actually owe. They continue to collect debt and the problem becomes so severe that they lose track of who they have to pay. This leads to them forgetting or underestimating how much debt they owe, which in turn only adds to their anxiety when new bills come or debt collectors begin to call. In order to assess your situation, you are going to need to calculate how much debt you currently owe. So get all your debt statements available for the next step. We are going to have you calculate how much credit card debt, government debt, and other debt you may owe.

Assessing Your Credit Card Debt

The first type of debt that we are to tackle is credit card debt. Credit card debt is one of the worst types of debt that you can have due to the extremely high interest rate. Unfortunately, this is the type of debt that most people abuse. Credit card debt is actually very easy to calculate, as your debt amount will be displayed on your monthly bill. Take all your credit card debt and separate them into columns. Have the amount you currently owe and next to that figure write in the current interest rate. Then calculate how much total credit card debt you owe by adding all the figures up.

Assessing Living Situation Debt

The next type of debt that we are going to discuss is your living situation debt. This is all the debt that you carry in order to maintain your living situation. For example, your mortgage, car payments, and furniture or electronic debt. This type of debt is not as bad as credit card debt due to lower interest rates, but it still can be a burden. Calculate how much debt you owe for your living expenses and once again create a column for your debt amount and a column for your interest rate that you pay. Then at the bottom, add up how much debt you currently have attributed to your living situation.

Student Loan Debt

The next type of debt we are going to discuss is student loan debt. Student loan debt is a rising epidemic and is compounded by the fact that the student unemployment rate hovers around 50%. Student loan debt is much more manageable than other types of debt due to low interest rates and the variety of different options available for repayment plans. Write down all your different student loans in columns and their respective interest rates. Then add up all the student loan debt that you owe at the bottom.

Government Debt

Back taxes and debt you owe to the government also need to be considered. This is usually the debt that most people forget to include. Government debt can usually be resolved relatively easily as the IRS has numerous repayment programs for you to choose from. But you still need to account for it in your overall debt calculation.

Putting It All Together

The next step you want to take is to add up all your debt into one lump sum. Now you might be surprised at this final number, but remember to be honest with yourself. Usually the majority of people are overwhelmed and generally underestimate the amount of debt they owe. They are usually surprised with this number and are quite shocked. Take a deep breath and remember this is the first step of your freedom process. You now have an understanding of the task before you. From now on, your goal is to reduce this number down to zero. You can do it, as long as you commit yourself to the process.

Escaping Credit Card Disaster

It does sound extraordinary when we find out about the recession being over from economic experts. Nonetheless, banks are proclaiming that defaults in credit card will get worse as it will shortly arrive at an unparalleled record.

Charge Cards

The reason for this has been credited, by a report from Reuters, to the rate of unemployment climbing to a 26 year high of up to 9.7% in August. Tragically, the level of unemployment is anticipated to grow in excess of ten percent before the year's over. All things considered, there are proven ways that you can utilize in order to shield yourself from the downward spiral.

Firstly, you have to do away with those credit cards. They have a method for sinking you into debt. Rather, take out a debit card from your bank or business organization. This helps you take out cash from your account. In any case, you have to abridge your spending habits so you don't overdraw yourself into turning into a borrower to your bank.

Things could get confounded with various cards. Try to have one which you must convey only when making obvious buys. This is a security safety measure as purchasing on impulse has driven numerous individuals into debt problems. If you're unsure whether you would be making needful buys, letting your card rest at home is better.

Request that your card firm puts your limit on the low side as well as your rate. Permitting a high limit is a surefire factor in purchasing on impulse for individuals who have no discipline. Never allow more than you can pay back at the end of the month to be on your card. Except for safeguarding your card balance, it additionally protects you from paying interest, as numerous firms don't put the rate up if you keep such habits.

Don't neglect to keep a watchful eye on changes to the terms and policies of your card. Particularly, watch out for changes with respect to minimum payments needed of cardholders and interest rates as well. Whenever you see that your card interest rate has increased, it is in your interest to find a lower premium card for yourself. You don't have to place high interest on your shoulders. Keep in mind, keeping a finer credit helps in qualifying you for lower rates.

Do you have reward cards? Then you should take extra caution with them, most users utilize these cards to their own detriment. This happens when they take more than the value of the card because of lack of attention to the expenses and rates that go with their credit card. Envision what you stand to gain by keeping to these points to the letter. Better still, I think the time is now time to investigate how you can save money on gas. Yes! It will truly stun you the extent to which you have been giving out what you could have been putting into building your cash tree.

Chapter 4: The Benefits of Money Management–Stopping the Madness

After my epiphany at the grocery store, I realized that I wasn't "too good" for all those jobs that I'd turned my nose up at in the wanted ads. The first thing I did after my trip to the library was rework my resume, tone down my ego, and go out and apply for as many jobs as I possibly could. Nothing was off limits, as I realized that having any amount of money coming in was better than the ZERO that had been coming the last few months.

It was about three weeks later when I got the call. I'd been offered a position. It just barely brushed up against my field and past experience and was a much more junior position that paid about a third of what I had been making previously. And yet, I was more grateful for that opportunity than almost any that I had been given previously. Hunger truly is the best sauce.

Now that I had some money coming in, I needed to decide what to do with it. The key word in that sentence is "decide".

Conscious Thought vs. Reactive Spending

Before this moment, I typically never gave money a second thought. It came into my account, and I spent it when and how I pleased. It doesn't matter how much money you make. If you don't think about your money, if you don't consciously decide what the best uses of it are, and most importantly if you don't create a PLAN for your money, then you will find it constantly slipping through your fingers.

This was brought into stark focus for me when I got my new job, because I had so much less money coming in than I was used to. This is when I started learning about budgeting.

Budgets: An Introduction

So, what is a budget? Essentially, it is a plan for your money. You'll read a lot of complicated explanations and descriptions of budgets in a lot of money-related books, but the truth is that a budget is simply a plan for your money. Once you know how much money you have coming in, you make a plan for how you will spend, invest or save it.

We'll get to the nitty-gritty of how to put together a budget and how to make budgeting simple in the later chapters, but for now, let's look at WHY budgeting your money is so important.

First of all, knowledge is power. That might be a bit of an old chestnut, but it's the truth, especially when it comes to money. The problem is that so many of us don't know where our money goes. It's the problem of the "latte generation", where people just keep spending $5, $10, or $20 on the incidental little purchases of day-to-day life. When you're not even aware of how or where you're spending your money, how can you possibly expect to control it?

Creating a budget gives you knowledge. It lets you clearly articulate how much money you have coming in, and where it is going out. This immediately puts control of your finances back in your hands. Maybe, if you're like me, this will be the first time in your life that you're really in control of your own money.

Basic Benefits of Budgeting

There are many benefits to learning to manage your money properly. For me, the top 5 were:

1. Regaining a Sense of Control
2. Strategically Coping With Debt
3. Being Able to Build a Savings Plan
4. Capping Impulse Spending
5. Focused Goal Achievement

Regaining Control

When my great collapse began, it was essentially because I felt like I had no control over my finances whatsoever. I had no real sense of how much things were costing me. This was especially true when it came to interest – I had no IDEA how much interest was accumulating on my debt each month when I was only making minimum payments on my balances.

When you've got a budget, and when you're actively managing your money, suddenly, you're in control of everything. You're in control of how fast your debt gets paid off. You're in control of your house, your car, your credit rating and how fast you can achieve your goals. When you've suffered a job loss or financial distress, the sense of empowerment that you can regain by taking ACTIVE control of your financial well-being is worth a great deal.

Strategically Coping With Deptostrofy

Debt is a reality for almost everyone living in this country. Unless you're in that elite 1% that doesn't need to borrow a cent, chances are you're in debt to someone. There are many different kinds of debt, and we'll get into that in a little more detail later on, but essentially there are "good debts" and "bad debts". All debt, whether or good or bad, needs to be managed.

By creating a budget and actively managing your money, you can come up with strategies to cope with debt actively, and create a plan for paying it off as soon as possible. Even if you have to live with "good debt" you can create plans for minimizing the interest that you pay. Interest is one of the absolute most insidious ways that our money disappears, and we'll look at a lot of different ways to minimize its impact on our lives.

A Savings Plan

This is a BIG ONE. When I was rolling high in what I sometimes call my "previous life" I didn't have a savings plan. In truth, I didn't even have a savings account. I just let all the money pile up in my account and then spent it. Most days I couldn't even have told you how much was in there.

Savings are a critical component of financial well-being, and it doesn't have to be a horrible burden. By getting strategic and creating a plan, you can make saving so painless that you barely notice it. However, you can also make it EFFECTIVE, so that you will be quietly growing your nest egg every single day of the year.

Capping Impulse Spending

We live in a world where impulse spending is encouraged everywhere we turn. In fact, impulse spending is so much more dangerous now than it was even ten years ago.

Think of all the ways you can spend money without thinking about it.

- You grab a coffee from a high-end coffee store on your way to work: $6
- You click a button on your phone to buy an app: $5
- You grab the magazine stacked by the till: $5
- You 'upsize' your meal at a fast food restaurant: $2
- You purchase a snack while at a sporting event: $8
- You buy a lottery ticket in passing: $5
- You grab lunch instead of going home or eating your packed lunch: $15

There are many people who will do several of this EVERY SINGLE DAY. I was certainly one of them. Looking back on my statements from the months before I lost my job, I can see that there were many days where I spent as much as $25 on impulse purchases alone.

Imagine that projected over the long term. That's $175 per week. Even scarier, that's $750 per month! That's what some people pay in rent! Or, to truly see how bad this is, you could project that kind of spending over an entire year.

The result is that you would have spent $9125 on impulse purchases. There are many high-quality used cars you could buy for that much money. Obviously this is an extreme projection, and in most cases it isn't really this bad. However, imagine even having an extra $3000 or $2000 in your bank account at the end of the year. Would you trade a few lattes and other impulse purchases for that money? I sure would. And did. And my life has never been better.

Goal Achievement

Some people think that managing your money, creating a budget, and saving means that you'll never get to have any fun with your money. I've discovered that it is the exact opposite. In fact, it is GREAT to have goals for fun things that you want to do with your money, like taking a vacation or buying that new TV.

The difference is that this way, you'll actually get to enjoy what you buy when you reach your goals! I bought many of the things I thought I wanted, and systematically had them taken away because they weren't really mine! They belonged to the bank, or the credit card company, or the store, and after I lost my job, I had no means to pay for them.

When you set a goal as part of a money management strategy, you will slowly put money away until you can achieve one of your goals, like taking that trip to Disneyland with your family. The best part is when you achieve it, you won't pay for it on credit, you won't pay interest on the trip, and you'll be able to really, truly enjoy it, because you will have worked hard to save up and achieve the goal.

Ultimate Benefit: MORE Money

Really, if you skipped the whole chapter and jumped to this section, I hope that it would be enough to convince you to start actively budgeting and managing your money. The number one reason to create a budget is that if you do it, you will ultimately have MORE MONEY. You'll have more money by the end of the first month that you put it into action, and more importantly, for the rest of your life.

There are probably millions of people in this country alone who have less money than they could, simply because they haven't taken a proactive approach to financial health. They let it slip through their fingers, pay outrageous interest and fees, and never put their money to work for them.

By taking even a few of the steps outlined in this book and putting them into practice, you CAN HAVE more money, without needing to earn any more, because you'll be making the best use of what resources you have. Of course, if you CAN earn a little more, even better, and we'll have some tips on that later on in the book!

Chapter 5: How to Recognize Bad Advice

Many financial advisors will discourage you from paying off your home mortgage early. They have many reasons for maximizing your portfolio and their profit with money you could have used to pay off debt. Let's cover the two most common ones.

It's Your Last Great Tax Write-Off

If you hit a patient's patellar tendon with a rubber hammer, the patellar reflex causes their leg to kick out. If you mention paying off your mortgage early, the tax write-off justification will automatically be mentioned. It's a reflex answer.

Never forget the only way to write anything off your taxes is to lose the money (i.e., pay it to the bank in interest). The rewards for your losses are less than you have been led to believe.

To use Dr. Morehouse's situation as an example: Let's assume she is married and filing jointly, so her 2016 standard deduction is $12,600. That means the first $12,600 of her Schedule A deductions don't even count. Everyone gets the standard deduction, even if they have nothing to deduct. Only the portion greater than the standard deduction creates a financial benefit. Also, if Dr. Morehouse is very productive and earns more than $309,900, her itemized deductions will be limited even more. The better you do financially, the less write-off you are allowed. If that's your last great tax write-off, I hate to think about the lesser ones.

Looking at Dr. Morehouse's $600,000 mortgage, the first year's interest will be $31,800. If she has no other deductions to take and doesn't make more than $309,900, then subtracting the standard deduction leaves an effective $19,200 write-off ($31,800 - $12,600). Assuming she pays a 40% combined state and federal tax rate, the $19,200 write-off will save $7,680 in taxes or 24% of the $31,800 she paid in interest to the bank. For every $100 paid to the bank in interest, the government will give Dr. Morehouse back $24. Even if she could get the full amount of interest as a deduction, it would only generate $40 in refund for every $100 deducted (lost). If you think that is a great deal, then feel free to send me the $100 instead of giving it to the bank and I'll be happy to return $80! That would be twice as good as the write-off.

Dr. Morehouse is better off keeping the $100 and paying the government $40 in taxes. She will have $60 in her pocket instead of $24. She is out more money by paying interest than by paying taxes. For every $100 she earns that's spent on interest, she will keep $24 after the deduction. The same $100 kept in her pocket will cost her $40 in taxes, leaving $60 available to spend. So what would Dr. Morehouse prefer to keep for her hard-earned $100: $60 or $24? Dr. Morehouse should pay the mortgage off early and keep the money. She earned it!

Interest Deduction

Keeping the Low-Interest Mortgage And investing for a Higher Return.

This is the second reason most commonly used for not paying off the mortgage early. If everything goes perfectly according to plan:

- You don't spend any of the money you were supposed to invest,
- Your investments get a higher return than the mortgage interest rate you are paying,
- You don't lose your job while you still have a mortgage,
- And the planets all align . . .

When all of the above work out, you could make a little bit of money off the interest difference between the mortgage and the investments. So, this one has a smidgen of truth to it, but it's far from a sure thing and very risky.

Why not go for the sure thing and the peace of mind? I have never encountered anyone who was sorry they paid off their home mortgage early. If someone were to pay off their mortgage early and become the first person to ever regret it, then they could always refinance the house and be back where they started.

I know one family who paid off their mortgage and then, a few years later, they took out a new mortgage to do some home improvements and buy an RV. It didn't take long before they regretted going back into Deptostrofy. They didn't repeat that mistake when they paid off the mortgage early the second time.

I've seen several physicians go through a tough time at the office and, through no fault of their own, had a drop in income. During this time, they were unable to make their mortgage payments and lost their houses. This would not have been the outcome if they had paid off the mortgage and actually owned their houses when their income fell.

Would anyone consider taking out a second mortgage on their house, adding to the risk of foreclosure, in order to invest the money in the stock market? For most of us the answer is no. When put like that it even sounds silly.

If we keep the low-interest loan and invest it for a higher return, we are effectively doing just that. We're borrowing against the house and putting it at risk to buy stocks. I have heard this referred to as the Low-Interest Dilemma. I don't see a dilemma. Pay off the house—don't use it as a piggy bank. It is your home, not an investment or leverage. Your personal house never shows up in the investment section of a budget, always in the expense section. Your goal is to minimize expenses.

Smoking five cigarettes is not as bad as smoking twenty. Likewise, paying 4% interest is not as bad as paying 10%. But make no mistake, the 4% interest and the five cigarettes are both still bad—but not as bad as the higher alternative. Lowering the interest rate does not make paying interest good, but it will cost less. Anytime compound interest is working against you, it's bad. Anytime compound interest is working for you, it's good. If it's working against you, the lower the interest, the better. Strive for the best though, which is zero interest.

This reminds me of the story of a police officer who ticketed a man for rolling through a stop sign. The man explained to the officer how he had slowed way down and that was effectively the same as stopping. It was close enough. The officer began to hit the man on the thigh with his baton. The man yelled for the officer to stop. The officer asked if he should stop or slow down since they were effectively the same. The message got through. We need to stop paying interest, not slow down or reduce the interest. Lower interest is better, but not the best.

People who use this strategy of investing rather than paying off their mortgage tend to continue this pattern indefinitely. Every few years, they refinance for a better rate, to purchase a bigger house or to harvest equity. Their mortgage tends to grow with time. Eventually they find themselves ready to retire with a larger mortgage than when they started. They never make headway and are paying interest and risking their home for their entire life.

The interest slowly eating away your wealth is like that seemingly innocuous drive-through drink you buy every day. You think it is only 500 calories, so it's no big deal. Five hundred calories, seven days a week, is 3,500 calories—which equates to one pound of fat. After a year, that little drink will add 52 pounds to your waistline and lighten your wallet by $1,600.

Paying off the mortgage also creates more cash flow in the current spending plan. If Dr. Morehouse did not have a mortgage, she would have an extra $3,332 available to spend each month. If her budget becomes tight, this could make a big difference.

One client of mine, I'll call him Dr. Green, was following the principle of investing instead of paying off his low-interest mortgage. He came to me to discuss his pending retirement. He planned to retire after five more years of investing and wanted my confirmation he was on track. After looking over his financial position, I suggested he take some of his savings and pay off his mortgage. If he didn't have the mortgage to pay, he already had enough money saved to cover his other expenses in retirement. He was planning to work five more years to have enough saved in his retirement account to retire with a mortgage. Eliminating the payment eliminated the need for more savings. He went home and talked it over with his wife, then paid off the house and retired one month later. Sometimes the answer is right in front of you, but you can't see it.

As time goes by, the balance owed on your mortgage drops and the payoff amount becomes smaller, but the monthly payment stays the same. The older the mortgage, the better your percentage return in cash flow is if you pay it off.

If Dr. Morehouse were down to her last $100,000 of principal on her mortgage, she would eliminate a $3,332 monthly payment with her $100,000 mortgage payoff. That $3,332 would be money in her pocket, each month, or almost $40,000-a-year guaranteed cash flow. Where else could she put $100,000 and generate a guaranteed $40,000 cash in hand the first year? If she made 8% on an investment, the $100,000 would generate $8,000 before taxes. Most doctors would prefer their spending plan had the extra $40,000 to utilize, especially if they are nearing retirement.

When you choose to gamble in the stock market for a higher return than the interest you are paying on your home mortgage, you are presuming on the future. It sounds good on paper, but it's not a sure thing. Your returns can be lower than expected. You could lose your income and then lose your home. If you don't have a mortgage, your house won't be at risk if your income falls.

Everything always looks good on paper. New ventures never go out of business on paper, yet 80% fail. No one goes bankrupt on paper, yet it happens all the time. No one loses their job on paper, yet I have seen physicians fired at a moment's notice. Many physicians have lost their homes because they couldn't keep up with the payments. Don't become one of the statistics.

When you pay off your house, you are getting a sure thing. When you invest in the market, you are taking a chance and betting you will make money; often you do, but not always. It's a risk you don't need to take. You will sleep better knowing your home is secure and the title is yours.

People use many other reasons/excuses for keeping the mortgage and stretching it out as long as possible, but they don't usually consider the total cost spread out over a lifetime. You will only generate a finite amount of earnings in your lifetime. Strive to give up as little as possible to the bank in the form of interest, thus keeping the maximum for your lifetime personal use and investing. Borrowing money to play with today means there will be even less to play with tomorrow.

Conflicts Of Interest

Often the people who are advising you to stretch out the mortgage have a conflict of interest when giving the advice. The advisor who makes money on your investment decisions is like the pharmaceutical rep who is telling you all about his new medication and why it is better than what you already use. The advice might be fine, but due to the obvious bias/conflict of interest, you never know when information is tipped in their favor. When you read a study about a new wonder drug and notice the manufacturer financed it, you tend to take the information with a grain of salt. Use the same skepticism with your financial advisors. Follow the money. Many a doctor has dropped his financial advisor after discovering the advisor was making more money off the portfolio than the doctor was.

Let's take a look at who is offering this advice.

The banker: If the bank holds your mortgage, they will continue to make a profit as long as you keep the mortgage and continue to pay interest. If the bank sells their mortgages, they make money by writing new loans (points, loan origination fee, and setup fees), so they would profit if you refinance and harvest some equity. If a competing bank holds the mortgage, then any money sent to the other bank to pay off that mortgage will not be available for you to deposit in a savings account or certificate of deposit in their bank, which your banker could loan out to make even more money. He is biased and has no reason to encourage you to pay off your house. He makes no profit if you pay off your house.

Stockbroker: A commissioned broker only makes money when you buy and sell stock. The more he can convince you to churn your account, the more money he makes. If you use your available cash to pay off a mortgage, that money will not be available to buy more stock and pay his fees. He is biased and has no reason to encourage you to pay off your house.

Insurance salesperson: Many of the insurance products they peddle are great for the insurance company and the salesperson's commission but are bad for you, the buyer. This is true for any kind of life insurance that is also an investment. Commissions come directly out of your pocket and are not available for the investment. Like the other listed advisors, if you use your available cash to pay off the mortgage, it will not be available to buy the overpriced, high-commission policy he wants to sell. (Only buy term life insurance and never use insurance as an investment.) He is biased and has no reason to encourage you to pay off your house.

Advisor paid on total portfolio: Some advisors are paid a percentage of your total portfolio value. The larger the balance in your investment account, the larger the advisor's paycheck. If you use your money to pay off your house, it is not in your portfolio to raise his income. He is biased and has no reason to encourage you to pay off your house.

Accountant: Many accountants are really tax preparers in disguise. You do need to have a top-notch accountant/CPA, not simply a tax preparer. Tax preparers may not be after what is best for you overall, but rather what creates the most deductions. The more tax deductions they can put on your tax return, the more it looks like they are earning their fee. "See what I did for you." Unfortunately, the things that create the most deductions are not always the best options.

Deductions are good, but only if you had to spend the money anyway. Remember, the reason you can claim a deduction is because you've lost money. As mentioned before, to lose one dollar in interest and gain 24 cents in tax refund is not a good deal by itself. To get the 24-cent refund for something you already had to pay anyway is a better deal. You don't have to pay mortgage interest. If you didn't have anything to deduct, you might not need someone to prepare your taxes. An accountant is less biased than the others, but has no motivation to encourage anyone to pay off their house.

Unbiased advisor: An unbiased advisor will not be selling anything or making any profit based on the decisions you make or the size of your portfolio. This person has your best interests in mind. If you do well, you tell your friends and he gets more clients. He has no biases to keep him from recommending that you pay off your mortgage, if it's in your best interest. This is the financial planner who is paid a fee for his time, not a commission or percentage of anything. This is the advisor you need to find.

Except for the unbiased advisor, the preceding examples are often salespeople masquerading as financial planners. They have their own best interests in mind and if they can help you along the way, that's a bonus. Some are legitimately trying to help you, but only in as much as it helps them too.

When I first set up my IRA during my internship, I went to an investment firm. The advisor helped me set up my IRA. The mutual fund he recommended had the highest front-end load allowable by law. In other words, it was the investment option making him the most money. He was only steering me to the investments that were lucrative for him.

I haven't had a home mortgage since October 2001. Compound interest has been working for me and not against me all that time. So how would Dr. Morehouse be affected if she did the same? Conventional Plan A would be to pay off her mortgage over 30 years with no refinancing or harvesting of equity. This would mean she would pay about $1.2 million over the 30 years ($600,000 in interest) and would have no additional savings.

In Plan B, she made extra monthly payments at first, paid off the mortgage over seven years, and then put the regular house payment of $3,331.83 into her retirement plan, which is invested in the stock market at an 8% average return over the next 23 years. She will pay $720,000 in the first seven years ($120,000 in interest) and own her house. Then the extra money she was paying toward the mortgage is put back into her lifestyle. The $3,331.83 a month original mortgage payment, invested for the remaining 23 years, would result in a $2,627,918 balance.

Plan A at 30 years = house paid off and no investments.

Plan B at 30 years = house paid off and $2,627,918 invested.

I'll take plan B where compound interest is turned around to work for me as soon as possible. In fact, that is exactly what I did. The security you feel when you have no mortgage is hard to quantify. The extra days you can take off from work without a mortgage are fun to enjoy and hard to quantify.

I hope these numbers help make the case for paying off your mortgage early. You work hard for your money. The bank doesn't deserve to have it more than you do!

Chapter 6: New Perspectives on Debt and Housing

Owning Too Much House Can Cripple Your Finances

It's easy to get caught up in the house-buying frenzy and end up with too much house for your budget, making you house poor. After so many years of depriving yourself during your training, when you finally start making money you feel you deserve a nice house. But at what cost? Does having five acres instead of one really make you happier? Will 5,000–10,000 square feet improve your well-being more than 3,500 square feet? If you bought the house for your family, but then you stay at work late to earn the money to pay for it and never see them, who are you kidding?

If you are overextended with too much house, there won't be enough money left for all the other things you need and would like to have. What will you have to eliminate? The dream car? New clothes? Vacations? Your retirement savings? Your children's college fund? Make no mistake; the extra money will have to be pulled from something. Is it really worth the trade?

How will it feel when you tell your children you would like to help them with their college costs, but instead you put the money into your expensive house? Did they enjoy the yard more than they would enjoy a college education without debt? Did you? Did your children enjoy going on vacation without one of their parents, who had to stay home working to make the house payment?

When I get ready to take a patient to surgery, I explain the procedure, alternatives, and risks. Only after I'm certain they understand what they are getting into, will I be satisfied if they decide to opt out of a needed surgery.

The same goes for your house purchase. Make sure you have counted the costs, checked the procedure, alternatives, and risks, and realized what you will be giving up to have that house. Otherwise, after buying too much house for your budget and struggling financially for the rest of your life, you may look back with regret.

A Few House-Buying Tips

1. Buy a house only when it fits into the plan. If that means renting while getting on firm financial footing (e.g., not drowning in debt), that's OK. Expanding your lifestyle slowly will allow you to get all the pieces in place before committing to the house payment. If you commit too soon, before you have accounted for everything in the spending plan—like disability insurance payments, for example—you may find yourself with too little money left to get everything you need. If you buy too soon, you may not be able to pay off your student loans quickly, and will pay unnecessary interest on them for years.
2. Don't buy a house as a resident or new attending. Wait until you know you are in a practice you'll want to stay in for more than five years. Avoid the forced sell at the end of residency, or if you discover you don't like the job you picked. The market might be down and you don't need the extra hassle at that point in your life.
3. Don't take on a home mortgage greater than two and a half times one spouse's or partner's income. This will leave plenty of space in the spending plan for all the other things life throws at you. It also keeps the two-wage-earning family safe if one of them loses their job. If you are in a higher-paying specialty, use an even lower multiple of your income.
4. Don't buy a house to keep up with the Dr. Joneses; buy a house that meets your needs. The Dr. Joneses of the world are getting into Deptostrofy —you don't want to be like them. Fully understand what you need and what you can afford, and let those issues guide you more than what you want and what the bank will loan you.
5. Pay off the mortgage as fast as possible, and then start earning interest instead of paying interest. The quicker you turn interest around and have it work for you instead of against you, the quicker you will reach your financial goals.
6. Never think of your personal residence as an investment. It's an expense. Always work to minimize expenses. If you think of it as an investment, it will taint your decision. You may get a bigger house

to make a better investment, and the added accompanying expenses could push you into bankruptcy and foreclosure.
7. Never treat your house like a piggy bank, harvesting equity or taking a second mortgage to buy something. No car, boat, motorcycle, motorhome, or any other toy is worth putting your home at risk. None of those things feels as good as being debt-free.
8. Never get an adjustable-rate mortgage. It's not worth the risk. Many people have lost their houses because of interest rate increases. Most people stretch their budget to the max to buy a house, leaving no room for the adjustable rate to adjust the payments higher. When it happens, you may end up in foreclosure.
9. If you find your house is too expensive and is choking out your spending plan, sell it. It is not worth the trouble it is causing you. The sooner you make the move, the better. It's only a building; you can find another one. One that fits into your income better and creates much more happiness.

Never let a house become a ball and chain attached to your leg. Make it instead a sanctuary of peace and tranquility.

Debt is Often an Unnecessary Risk

Every doctor has experienced that patient. The one with so many medical problems and medications that you don't understand how he can still be alive. But there he is, sitting on the exam table, seeking your help.

Mine was a 65-year-old white male with alcoholic cirrhosis, ascites, COPD, diabetes, atrial fibrillation, hypertension, and—among other things—congestive heart failure. He had a list of medications longer than my arm, including prednisone for his lungs and Coumadin for his atrial fibrillation. He was in the resident clinic and I was a fourth-year surgery resident, working him up for his painful umbilical hernia. It was large but not incarcerated.

He told me, "Doc, you've got to do something. I don't like having this thing sticking out in front of me. It bugs me."

I finished the examination and presented the case to my attending, who asked what I thought we should do. I said it would be a risky surgery, but he was complaining about it so I thought we should fix the hernia. He leaned back in his chair and said something to me I never forgot:

Don't poke a skunk.

"Even though he might have some symptoms with the hernia, the situation might be made worse if we take him to the operating room. He is likely to have complications and may not even survive the surgery. He has been living with the hernia up until now; he can live with it a bit longer. Don't poke a skunk."

That moment was burned into my memory. I've been in similar situations since and the conversation keeps coming back to me. Don't poke a skunk.

If you poke a skunk, you might get away with it and you might not. You might have a great story to tell or you might end up soaking in a tomato juice bath tonight. It's a risk you don't need to take.

Several years ago, my family started riding quads (all-terrain vehicles) in the Oregon sand dunes. One day, we came upon a lake in the dunes. One side of the lake was right up against a cliff of sand about 100 feet tall. People riding along the side of the cliff with their quads could look to the left, down the cliff, and see the water. Looking to the right, up the cliff, is the sky. It looked like a great thrill. My kids wanted to do it. This was a good teaching moment. I told them, "Don't poke a skunk."

They didn't get it. So I explained to them, even though it may be a lot of fun and a great adrenaline rush, the consequences of a mistake were high. I said, "If you hit a bump and your thumb touches the kill switch, you and your quad are going swimming. If your quad quits on the side of the hill or runs out of gas, you and the quad are going swimming."

So they commenced to explain to me how those things rarely happened and since it was unlikely to happen, it should be OK. Since it was me who was paying for the quad, it would be no skin off their nose if it went swimming. Dad would fix it. When I told them they would be responsible for the $2,000 it would take to repair the quad after a swimming trip, there was a lot less interest in riding the side of that hill.

The likelihood of a bad outcome should not drive our decision. The consequences should prevail.

Yes, falling in the lake had low odds, but if it did happen, it would be very expensive. And it did happen: every month we saw someone who had fallen into the lake being towed back to the campground. Don't poke a skunk. It's a risk you don't need to take.

Acquiring and maintaining debt is also a risk you don't need to take. Most of the time, you can get away with it. You have been getting away with it for many years, as you borrowed your way through medical school. You may get away with it, if you buy a house that stretches your spending plan or a car you really can't afford. Then one day, when you're not paying close enough attention, or something you hadn't planned on occurs, you will find yourself in a financial mess that wouldn't exist had you avoided the debt in the first place. Don't poke a skunk. It's a risk you don't need to take.

When you borrow money, you are presuming on tomorrow.

Whenever you borrow money, you have committed to using some of next year's income to pay for this year's indulgence. What if next year doesn't go as planned? What if your finger happens to touch the kill switch? What if pregnancy comes around a little sooner than planned and morning sickness makes it impossible to work? What if a fall on a hiking trip fractures a few bones, and results in a six-month disability? What if Congress passes a new law that makes it unprofitable for hospitals to employ doctors? No one ever knows when a stroke is coming, as it did for one of my internal medicine friends. His career came to a sudden and unexpected end.

The future holds many uncertain and unknown events. When you borrow money, you are assuming your circumstances will continue unchanged, and you will be able to pay off your loan with future earnings. Isn't that why you borrowed money in medical school? You assumed your income would be greater as an attending and you could pay all the money back then. What if your career path changes? What if your dream changes from joining a private practice to becoming a village doctor at a medical mission hospital in a third world country? With all that debt to pay, such an option may be off the table. What if a parent has a stroke and they need you close by for help, but they live in a depressed small town where doctors aren't paid so well? What if your parents need to move into assisted living on your dime? What if your sister and her husband die in an accident and you are suddenly raising two more children? If you have too much debt, you may limit your options or face financial hardship.

On the other hand, what if you were debt-free when any of these events occurred? You can be open to making all kinds of moves if you don't have any debt.

Debt can severely limit your lifestyle choices.

I know several physicians who are feeling burned out. They need to back away from their practice and take some time off to pull themselves together. They need some recuperation time and maybe even a sabbatical—but debt is making it impossible to decrease their work hours. Options are lost. They poked the skunk and the skunk won.

During the housing market crash in the late 2000s, many people declared bankruptcy or gave their houses back to the bank. Why did that happen? Their income usually didn't change. Their mortgage payments didn't change (unless they were foolish enough to fall into the adjustable-rate mortgage trap). Yet they were walking away from their houses.

Many of them refused to pay more money for a house than it was worth. If the mortgage was greater than the house value, they walked away. It ruined their credit rating and their reputation. The irony of the decision was they already had agreed to pay way more for the house than it was worth when they agreed to pay interest for 30 years.

One friend in the construction business built multiple houses that he had floated on loans. When the housing crash happened, his business was so upside down he saw no other way out but to take his own life. Presuming upon tomorrow cost him his life. He was borrowing money during the good times, expecting the good times to continue. There will always be both good years and bad years. Your plans need to work for both.

Plan as if next year will be a good year, and you will go bankrupt if you are wrong. Plan as if next year will be a bad year, and you can enjoy it, good or bad.

Bankruptcy and debt go hand in hand. The more debt you carry, the higher the chance something will happen to push you into bankruptcy. You fall into the lake with your quad.

During the 1990s, this country had a great economic boom. Here was a chance to get ahead financially, pay off debt, and stuff a lot of money into retirement accounts. The same chance was available to the government, as everyone paid higher taxes with the increased prosperity. But that's not how it turned out.

During that very prosperous time, many were spending their money as fast as they could make it, and then some. Debt was climbing when debt should have been decreasing. People presumed on tomorrow and borrowed even more. Times were good and getting better, so they assumed they would have even more money next year. Borrowing and spending maxed out. Credit card debt climbed. Mortgage debt climbed. Car debt climbed. They forgot about this time-tested wisdom:

Make hay while the sun shines.

When times are good, resist the temptation to spend and borrow. Good times are the best times to be saving, getting ready to weather future storms. Fill the loft with hay, so you can feed the cows in the winter when the grass is snow-covered. Pay off your debts. Put money into your savings and retirement accounts. Pay off your house. Then when the bad times hit—and they will—you will be ready to weather the storm.

When the housing bubble broke, many people went bankrupt. Contractors were stretched to the max and couldn't sell houses for enough to pay their debts. During a time when we, as a country, should have been in a great economic position, we spent the time sticking our necks out. Don't poke a skunk. It's a risk you don't need to take.

Had we shored up our finances in the 90s while prosperity abounded, the crash in the next decade wouldn't have amounted to much. We could have easily weathered the storm, because the hay would have been in the barn when winter set in. As with my cirrhotic hernia patient, there are risks you don't need to take. Don't poke a skunk. You might not like the results. Don't make this mistake. When you are doing well, pay off your debt; don't borrow more, expecting to continue to do well forever.

What If you're Drowning in Debt?

Some doctors are not merely in debt, they are drowning in debt. They are desperately looking for something to grab ahold of to keep from drowning. At this point, drastic measures are needed. A major change must take place to get back in balance. All efforts need to focus on debt reduction at this point.

I counseled one doctor who had a sudden and permanent drop in income and asked me what he should do. Looking over his spending plan revealed he was falling $5,000 further in the hole every month. A drastic change was needed and fast. I told him the only good option in his plan was to sell his lavish house and get a less expensive one. It was his riverside dream home and he wasn't interested in selling. But there was no other place to cut $5,000 a month. He went away dissatisfied with my advice. Six months later and another $30,000 in the hole, he put his dream house up for sale.

He had no other solution, yet it took another six months for him to come to grips with it. He sold the house quickly and moved into a less expensive house, and within three months of the decision, he had regained financial balance.

When you find yourself in a hole, stop digging.

- Will Rogers

When you are in a bad way financially, it will take a big move to correct it. Clipping coupons will not cut it. You may need to sell a house that is crushing you, or that new sports car you can't really afford. You may need to work additional shifts or take extra calls to make more money to improve the situation. In general, doctors do not have an income problem—they make good money. They usually suffer from an expense problem and are not willing to face it.

The biggest problem you will face is simply facing the problem.

I have counseled numerous doctors in financial dire straits, and often found things could easily be solved by changing to a less expensive house. Often that single move made them debt-free and able to restart their financial journey in a balanced and healthy fashion. Breathing room and peace of mind are within their grasp. Once they are out from under the burden of drowning debt, they are able to plot a course for success. Until they can come to grip with the true problem, they can't stop drowning.

Smokers don't quit smoking when you tell them to quit, they quit when they decide to quit. You can't get someone else to lose weight until they commit to that goal. Getting out of debt is the same. Until you personally make the decision to do it, it will not happen. However, once the decision is made, it is a simple process to accomplish. Your eyes are now open to the possibilities and you can begin making changes.

If you want something to change, you have to change something.

Make the decision to get your finances back under control, and it will happen. Doctors are smart people, and anyone who can survive medical training can do what it takes to become debt-free.

Part 3: Setting Financial Goals

Chapter 7: Make Your Plan

The most important aspect of getting out of deptostrofy for good is to create a proper game plan and make sure you follow it. The failure rate goes up dramatically for individuals who fail to plan properly. A strong game plan will allow you to always know what steps you need to take and exactly how you are going to achieve them. You will also be able to view your progress which allows you to celebrate little victories and really build confidence.

Building positive momentum in the beginning will allow you to create a sense of accomplishment and you will find that each step becomes easier and easier. Individuals without a plan may never know if they are making progress and will usually revert back to old habits. This chapter will be dedicated to creating a plan and exactly how you can execute it and get rid of debt once and for all.

Make Sure You Have Explored All Your Options

The first step you need to take in creating your game plan is to make sure you have explored all your options. We gave you a few suggestions in the previous chapter and hopefully you have researched and explored each of those scenarios. Understanding your options will allow you to tailor your game plan to your current situation. Having a reduced debt amount or lowered interest rates will allow you to change your game plan and overall goals. So before you proceed and really begin to drill down and create your game plan, make sure you have taken the time to explore all options available to you.

Analyzing Your Income

There is a chapter dedicated to creating more income later in this report, but in order to game plan properly we need to take a look at your current income statements. You need to gather all checks and cash flows that you receive on a monthly basis. Your income from your job and side jobs will all count as income. Most people will have a good idea how much they make during a month, but make sure you're accounting for every income stream possible. You want to calculate your income for each month and write that number down. You also want to account for any future cash flows that are coming.

Are you going to make more money in a few months? Extra income from investments? Try to calculate your income in six months. Now you need to remember to be honest with yourself and only record income that is guaranteed. Writing down that you are going to get a 10% raise in six months, would be nice, but it is not something that can be guaranteed. So calculate your income into two numbers: one for income now and another for income in six months.

If you think your income will decrease in six months then you need to write down that number as well. Remember the more detailed and honest you are with your assessment, the better your game plan will be.

Analyzing Your Expenses

The next step in creating your game plan is to analyze your expenses. For this step, we want to analyze your expenses with debt NOT included. Where does your money go each month? What are you spending your income on? This part needs to be as detailed as possible. Use credit card statements as a guide and break down all your expenses into different categories. If you use cash, you may need to record all your expenses for one month. Detail is crucial, as you need to understand exactly where your money is going month in and month out. This will help you resolve financial leaks and will also allow you to create a monthly budget. Add up all your expenses for the past few months and write down your average monthly expenses. Remember this number should be all your expenses without debt. Hopefully this number is less than your monthly income figure. Now that you have both income and expense numbers, we are one step closer to assessing your financial situation.

Add in the Debt

The final step to assess your situation is to add in the final number, minimum monthly debt. You want to add up all your minimum required monthly payments and add that number to your list. This number should be after you have explored your options, and you have concluded that this is the figure you need to pay. So your game plan should have three numbers: Income, Expenses, and minimum monthly debt payments. You want to add up all three totals and hopefully you have a positive number. If you don't we have ways to get you to break even in the next chapters.

Setting Aside a Fixed Number to Allocate to Your Debt

That positive number that you calculated above will now become your most powerful weapon to get rid of deptostrofy. You need to budget this fixed number each and every month and view it as a bill. Under no circumstances are you allowed to use this income for anything other than paying off your debt. Most people fail because they will change this number each month. They will put $500 towards debt one month, feel good about themselves, then only put $100 the next month. You need to make sure you keep this number fixed. If you pay off one of your debts completely, and now have extra cash, by all means increase this number. This will create a powerful snowball effect. The last thing you want to do is decrease this number. Decreasing your allocated debt cash number is a quick way to fail and not stick to your game plan.

Deciding Which Debt to Pay Off First

You are going to need to prioritize your debt and decide which debt you want to pay off first. There are generally two methods you can take in identifying which debt to pay off first. The first method recommends that you tackle the highest interest rate debt. High-interest rate debt, such as credit card debt, is technically costing you the most money. Your monthly payments may not be as high as your mortgage for example, but a 24% interest rate needs to be handled immediately.

The second method of paying off debt is to get rid of your smallest debt amounts first. This will allow you to slowly rid yourself of a debt, and take the money that you used to pay towards your old debt and allocate it to new debt. We recommend that you pay off the higher interest rates first, as mathematically that is the best way to cut your debt. Even though it may be rewarding to eliminate small debts, you will be saving yourself money in the long run by tackling your highest interest rates first. So if you have a positive cash flow each month, make sure you make the minimum payments on all your other debt, but apply the extra cash flow to the debt with the highest interest rate.

Setting A Time Frame

Having a time frame will allow you to keep track of your progress and you will be able to reward yourself after little victories. If you can project the amount of money that you are going to allocate to high-interest loans each month, you can predict how long it will take to pay off all your loans and become debt free. While we are not going to get into math calculations in this report, there are numerous debt calculators online that will help to figure out how long it will take to pay off debt with a fixed payment each month. The great thing about tackling high-interest rate debt first is that you will always be lowering your principal each month and paying less interest each month. So the more you pay off your loans, the less interest you have to pay, the more money you can then allocate to paying off that loan at a faster pace. This creates a snowball effect and once you get started it becomes easier and easier to pay off debt each and every month. The problem that most people face is they cannot stick with their game plan and they fail to make it through the crucial first months.

What If I Don't Have Extra Cash To Allocate To Debt?

If you find yourself working with negative numbers, don't sweat just yet. The next few chapters are going to deal with ways you can increase cash flow to allocate to debt. You need to really drill down on expenses and income. Is there anything you can cut? Can you increase income? Have you explored all options?

Create A New Financial System

Hopefully you understand everything I've discussed up until now, and that you have already or plan on implementing a lot of it in your life.

Right now, we're going to take a look at creating a completely new system for your finances, which is based on your monthly budget.

Why is a financial system beneficial?

It keeps track of every dollar coming in and going out of your pocket.

It allows you to commit the largest amounts of money to your debts right now, and even if you didn't have debt, it will allow you to commit the largest amounts of money to your investments, hobbies or vacations.

At the end of the day, achieving financial freedom isn't about how much money you make; rather, it's about how much money you keep. And at the most fundamental level, a financial system focuses on keeping more money in your hands after all of your expenses.

Create A Budget

Now that we have assessed our income and expenses on a monthly basis, and we have the ability to increase our income as much as possible, as well as decrease our expenses as much as possible, we can make a somewhat accurate budget that gives us solid estimations of monthly incomes and expenses.

This is exactly what I want you to do. You now have a lot more information than you had previously, so there is no reason why you cannot make a more accurate and reliable budget.

This budget will then be used to estimate future monthly incomes and expenses, and it will be used as the foundation of our financial system.

Remember you don't have to get it right the first time; you can always make changes as the months go on. With the financial system I present below, given a worst possible scenario, there are still funds you can access from your savings account again (debt payments occur after all expenses are incurred).

Emergency Fund

This is a quick interruption to the flow of this current step, but it's something I want to introduce and emphasize the importance of.

An emergency fund is essentially a separate bank account (usually a high interest online account) that holds cash that you have socked away for a "rainy day".

Ideally, we want about $1,000 in our emergency fund, and we only touch that in the case of an emergency.

Why is it important?

The main reason it's important is because it will hopefully be the funds you will use in replacement of your credit card. Usually when there's an emergency and you don't have enough money in your bank account, you'd put the charge on your credit card. This time, however, you will have this emergency fund to fall back on.

Honestly, at this current stage when paying off your debt is your largest priority, it's obvious that you can't just create an emergency fund and put $1,000 into it.

So, what I recommend is that you take 5% of your Wipe Out Money every month and put it to your emergency fund. Once the fund hits $1,000 you can put this 5% back to your Wipe Out Money and contribute it to your debt.

Monthly Financial System

We're going to take a look at this monthly financial system now, and the best way I recommend setting it up for the most benefit from your Wipe Out Money.

For this system to work fully, you need to have two bank accounts, a checking and a savings account. A third account will also be needed for your emergency fund. If you don't already have three accounts, you can contact your bank and get that sorted without any issues.

We are also assuming in this process below that you get paid a paycheck from your employer once a month. If you get paid weekly, biweekly, or inconsistently (from another income source) you can still apply this same process by choosing the same payday that occurs every month. For example, if you get paid every two weeks, simply pick the first payment of the month as your "Day One".

Now that you know this, we can get to the system.

1. Income

As mentioned several chapters ago, this includes all the money coming into your bank account. The money comes into your checking account on your payday (Day One) and that same day or the day after you have an automatic transfer that sends your Wipe Out Money automatically to your savings account.

If you haven't figured it out already, we have to assign the amount of our Wipe Out Money BEFORE the month begins to set this up automatically.

This means that after the Wipe Out Money is sent to the savings account, the amount left in the checking account will be exactly what we need to spend on our expenses for the month. This is where the accuracy and good estimation of our monthly expenses come into play (you can give yourself a little bit of buffer room and overestimate expenses slightly).

This is great for two reasons.

Firstly, you are paying yourself first, and by paying yourself first, you're ensuring your debt gets paid first.

Secondly, you are giving yourself an actual monetary limit. Having X amount of dollars in your account to spend on expenses will ensure you only spend X since you can't go over.

2. Expenses

If allowed, you want to automate as many of your bills as possible and get them set up to automatically deduct the payment from your checking account - this will save you time.

For any bills that can't be done automatically, for example, rent, you can go to an ATM and withdraw the cash for it.

For groceries, you can use a debit card that is attached to your checking account, or again, withdraw the cash out from an ATM.

The point is that your budget for expenses for the month was as accurate as possible so that you don't need to touch any of the Wipe Out Money in your savings!

If anything, hopefully you have some money left over before your next payday, after all expenses are paid. If this is the case, send this extra money also to your savings account, adding it to your Wipe Out Money.

3. Wipe Out Money

So right now, once all expenses are paid, you're left with your Wipe Out Money in your savings account, and that's it!

On the day before your next monthly payday, or two days prior to your next payday, you want to go through and do the following step.

4. Emergency Fund

Right before your next payday, send 5% of the amount in your savings account to ANOTHER savings account, which will act as your emergency fund account.

Hopefully this other account is a very high-interest rate account, gaining you the best interest on the money that sits there.

5. Wipe Out Money (minus 5%) Thrown at Debt

The remaining money in your first savings account will be your Wipe Out Money, and on your next payday (when you see the money in your checking account) send all of this Wipe Out Money to the first debt on your "Debt Sheet"!

The reason we wait until we get the money in our checking account is so that we always have access to money in case we ever need it for anything. Keep in mind that when our emergency fund is also established we will have another buffer of safety.

Now repeat the cycle every month with the new paycheck money. Remember that when your emergency fund has $1,000, you can either keep contributing to it if you want, or just skip that step and throw all your money to your debt.

Part 4: Taking Action

Chapter 8: Investing: The Secret to Financial Freedom

The ultimate secret to achieving financial freedom is through investments. Well placed investments are like seeds planted in fertile soil. They will grow into huge yields, which will in turn create more "seeds" to plant. This chapter will now show you the basic principle of investments, which can help anyone to find financial freedom and get out of Deptostrofy.

Types of Investments

According to economics, there are two main types of investments; ownership investments and lending investments.

What is an Ownership Investment?

Just as the term implies, ownership investments are the types of investments that are owned by the investor. The most common example of owned investments is having one's own business. Basically, millionaires got their millions from having owned investments.

Their salary is spent on well-placed investments by creating businesses.

Another term for this is "entrepreneurship." Entrepreneurship is arguably the most difficult type of owned investments, but it has the potential to provide unlimited yield. Bill Gates got his billions from his well-placed investment in his business named "Microsoft."

If one wants to have a good investment and get the financial freedom one wants, then own a business and start your own positive cash flow from the passive income your investment creates. These are the types of ownership investments that are trending today:

Online Business – this is arguably the fastest growing type of business today, especially due to the increased influence of the Internet in modern society. Having your own online business is not that difficult, especially if you have basic computer and Internet skills. The only technical requirement for this type of business is web designing (for the appearance of your website), and other various types of Internet optimization. Compared to traditional businesses, online businesses do not require a large start up, one only needs a good product, a computer and an Internet connection and you are good to go.

Real Estate – this type of investment relies on the increasing value of land, especially in areas that are industrialized and urban. However, this type of investment is not a fast cash option for people who want to have cash quickly. However, the returns for such an investment can be extremely high, as land value in urban areas can quadruple in value in just a couple of years. The downside to this type of investment is when land value depreciates, especially as centers of commerce may change location in time. What seems to be a hub of commerce today may become a deserted wasteland tomorrow, nobody can tell.

Entertainment – this is the most successful of all businesses today. Anything that involves entertainment is a sure win in investments. Every kind of entertainment business, from movies to local comedy bars, has a high rate of success, especially if the level of entertainment people experience is high.

Food Businesses – Food has always been a necessity in every society ever since man developed the idea of social belonging. It is the most diplomatic type of business available as people all over the world agree to eat tasty food. If you are a good cook, then the food business is the best investment you can have in your life.

Electronics – with the growing dependence of societies on electronic devices, a business focused on providing electronics will surely be successful. Aside from this, computer programming and software used to run these electronics also becomes an important necessity today.

Mobile Apps – with the rise in the use of smartphones, anything involving these amazing gadgets are good business. The mobile application or apps business is so profound that their mobile app developers become financially successful, literally in just one night. It is important to understand that this type of business requires advanced learning on computer programming and mobile app development.

If you happen to be interested in investing in businesses, the types of businesses indicated above are proven to be successful today. However, if you are not that keen to do business, then the other type of investment may be the perfect choice.

What is Lending Investment?

Lending investments are almost the same as ownership investments, but instead of placing your money in your own business, you are placing or investing your money in someone else's in the hope of returns. One of the best examples of lending investments is buying company stocks. Though this might be more risky compared to owning a business, it is not as difficult as owning a business. One can simply avail the service of a consultant in order to manage your investments.

Another lending investment is if one were to place money in a bank and have it accrue over time. This is nice when you have a large amount of money that you do not want to spend any time soon. However, if you do not have the money, then creating money through the first investment type, which is doing business, may be your only option. Remember to always keep in mind that the money you make is not only used to spend. It can also be used to generate more money and in turn be used to make more money and so on. Always remember that your money can work for you, but only if you let it do its job.

I hope that this small guide will help you achieve all of your dreams and help you become financially stable and free.

Happy investing and may you find freedom as soon as possible!

Chapter 9: Start Building Your Credit

When you apply for a credit card or other type of payment card, you will be subjected to a limit. The limit is designed to ensure that you do not go over a certain amount on your card. A creditor will impose a limit based on your history to ensure that the creditor will not be at risk of losing money to someone who might be a risk.

Your credit card limit is critical to your credit history and report. You need to have a high limit to ensure that you can have a better rating and you will have more spending power to work with. You must still avoid charging up to that limit or else you might be seen as a high-risk client, thus causing your score to go down some more.

What Determines Your Credit Card Limit?

There are many things that will determine your credit limit.

1. Your Credit Score

Your credit score is the most basic point that will determine what your credit rating will be. You will get a higher credit limit if your score is greater.

2. Your Income

Although your credit score will determine your credit limit, it is even more important that you can show that you have sufficient income to pay off that credit. Your income will be reviewed based on your tax returns and other details.

You will have to provide information on your income when applying for a card. This will be compared with information on your tax returns. When the credit card company considers your income they will determine a proper value for your credit based on what you can afford to pay off within a certain amount of time.

3. Your Repayment History

Your ability to pay off the card can influence what a creditor might consider after you have had the card for a period of time. The creditor might feel that you are indeed capable of paying off your debts on-time, thus allowing that creditor to give you a higher credit limit. This, in turn, improves upon your credit score even more.

4. Debt to Income Ratio

Your debt to income ratio refers to how much income you have versus the debts you accumulate. When you have more income and less debt, you are showing to a credit card company that you can manage your credit well and you will not get into Deptostrofy.

A good thing about your credit limit is that your creditor might take a look at your account on occasion to see that it works well. You might be able to get an increase after a regular check. Each card team will look at accounts at different times. A group might review accounts every six to twelve months, but others might wait a little longer.

No-Limit Cards Are False

When looking for a credit card, you might see something like a no-limit credit card. This gives the impression that you can spend as much on that card as you want.

Let's be realistic. Do you genuinely believe that someone would give you a no-limit card that will provide you with all the spending power you have ever wanted? There's no way that this would happen. The creditor would be at risk of letting you buy literally anything you want without any real consequences involved.

So, what is a no-limit card? A no-limit card is actually one that says there are no preset limits on the card. The limit is based on your spending habits. That total could be flexible depending on what you spend on it. There is a chance that the limit could be increased, but the good news is that the odds of the limit decreasing will be extremely minimal.

This is a trick that many credit card companies will use. They will market themselves as offering no-limit cards, but those cards will have real limits. They will just vary based on one's use. The card company will hide information about those limits in the fine print of the application.

Be aware of this when finding a good card that works for you and has a sensible limit. It might be easy for you to find a great deal on a card if you are careful and ask questions.

What You Can Do to Improve Your Credit Limit

It is clear that you should charge amounts close to your credit limit when using your card or else your credit limit will be at risk. If you increase that credit limit over time, it becomes a little easier for you to spend more money without going over that limit. It is better to have a limit of $5,000 while spending up to $2,500 on it than it is to have a limit of $3,000. Besides, having a higher limit shows that you are responsible with your money.

There are many things that can be done to increase your credit limit:

1. Make sure you make your payments regularly and on-time.
   This is the most important point as a few missed payments will surely ruin your credit score.
2. Use your line of credit for a longer period of time.
   Creditors typically provide long-term clients with better credit limits. They do this as a means of rewarding people for their loyalty.
3. Avoid adding more onto your card than necessary.
   Keep the balance owed under the 50% of your credit limit.
4. Contact the creditor after a while to see if you can get a higher credit limit.

Sometimes a credit card company will automatically provide you with a higher credit limit if you have done well enough with your existing one. This is not always the case, but it is a simple convenience that you will enjoy.

Ask For an Increase on Your Credit Limit

Getting a higher credit limit is a good way to help you repair your credit score. Many credit card companies are willing to give you a higher limit.

What to Consider Before Asking

Start your search for a higher credit limit by taking a look at your credit situation first.

1. Check on your credit score first.
   It will be easier to get an increase on your credit limit if your credit score has improved recently.
2. Think about why you need a higher credit limit.
   You might have to explain to the creditor why you want to increase your credit limit.
3. Think about how much credit you really need.
   You should be realistic when it comes to your request for an added credit limit. Avoid asking for a huge increase.

The Process of Asking

There are a few steps that can be used when asking for a better credit limit:

1. Check how you can contact the credit card company. You might go online, but you could also possibly send a request by mail.
2. Discuss your history of using your card.
   Talk about as many details about your card as possible. Describe how long you have had the card and how much time you have spent paying it off. Be sure to talk about your payment plans and that you have not gone beyond your limit.
3. Explain your finances if possible.
   You might mention that your income has increased dramatically recently. Do not mention other debts that you have.
4. Be direct and explain why you need to increase your credit limit.
   Be specific about what you plan on purchasing.
5. Never act desperate when requesting the credit increase.

6. Don't expect an immediate response.
    Be willing to spend a bit of time waiting to see if you will get a higher credit limit. The credit card company receives many requests, so be patient.

Be Aware of the Credit Check

Don't forget the credit check is a full view of your credit report. The credit check will cost a few points off your credit score, but it won't be much.

When Should You Apply For an Increase?

Do not bother asking for an increased limit for a new card. Credit card companies want to ensure that the people who use their cards make regular and on-time payments and work toward paying them off over a longer period of time. Do not ask for an increase on a card that is less than six months to a year old.

Can You Apply For a Card With a Higher Limit?

You have the option to apply for a new credit card that has a higher limit. That is not necessarily the best thing to do to improve your credit rating. There are many problems associated with doing this as they can impact your credit score:

- This would require another inquiry on your credit report, thus costing points on your rating.
- The fees associated with some high-limit cards may be too high.

You would have to pay annual fees on some of these cards. Sometimes a company might provide you with a fee-free service for the first year, but that might be to mask the high value of the fee after that year is up. Don't forget about the interest rates; these fancy cards might come with very high rates due to their limits being high. These high rates are to offset the risks associated.

- Many groups that offer high-limit cards are extremely selective about choosing their applicants.

- You might also be subjected to fees even when you do not use the card.

The fees in question might be small in value, but they can add up if you ignore your card. Many high-end companies, particularly luxury-oriented groups like American Express, might cause you to spend more than needed on your account.

Having a higher limit will increase your credit rating, but you must be aware of how you are spending money surrounding that limit.

Conclusion

Thank you again for downloading this book!

I hope this book was able to help you to tackle that debt head on and start your journey toward living a debt free life.

Getting into debt and having a bad credit score tends to be the result of weak financial practices. Thus, it's critical that you start cultivating superior economic habits as early as possible. Listed below are three of them as you can begin learning immediately:

Learn to budget

Overspending causes many debt issues. This is the place where a budget might help. You can be told by a budget how much you should be shelling out for each product in your life. This enables your financial life to remain organized.

You ought to begin to list most of the charges you've made. Including book, tools, food, personal care, travel, spending cash, amusement, passions, training, along with other things.

Then verify full spending against your income. If your earnings cannot help it or you rarely manage, you have to cut down on your costs.

You ought not to commit away from budget except if it is an urgent situation where a budget ought to be flexible.

Live within your means

If you should be getting $40k a year but have unpaid payments and extreme debt, it's time to improve your lifestyle. Numerous people have a very good credit rating and extremely small debt.

The easiest way to make sure that you have a superb credit rating - regardless of what your income - is always to invest less than you generate. That means living below your means. When you have very little money, you will need to reside with roommates so that you can keep down costs. If you have a medium sized income, that will imply saving more and engaging less.

Your earnings aren't a factor in identifying your credit rating but the method you use to control income, and your debts do. Even if you won the lottery, your credit rating would not be damaged. Remember, it is how you manage your cash that is the issue.

Save and Spend

Saving is one of the most efficient methods for making sure your credit score keeps in prime condition. It is because you will be prepared for financial problems and your money may grow. If you are in the practice of saving and reinvesting, it is unlikely you'll enter into the bad behavior of overspending. Damage to your credit score is very much reduced and so is your chance of stepping into debt.

You must get information on money management to enhance your knowledge. There are various easy and positive economic behaviors you can add into your daily life. The faster you do it, the easier your daily life is going to be.

Finally, if you enjoyed this book, then I'd like to ask you for a favor, would you be kind enough to leave a review for this book on Amazon? It'd be greatly appreciated!

Thank you and good luck!

Personal Finances Series

The series that grows with your financial healthiness. We hope that with us you are getting a little further in achieving goals and money Olympus.

1. Financial Management for Beginners: You Need a Budget to Manage Your Money. Personal Planning, Money Mindset and Discipline for Financial Independence
   by David Stokes
   (https://www.amazon.com/dp/B07B728RHY)
2. Overcoming Deptostrofy: A Complete Guide to Debt and Loans Management for Free Life Forever and Ever
   by David Stokes
   (https://www.amazon.com/dp/B07T8SZ8LW)

www.ingramcontent.com/pod-product-compliance
Lightning Source LLC
Chambersburg PA
CBHW030729180526
45157CB00008BA/3097